How to Drop Five Strokes without Having One

Other books by John D. Drake

Downshifting: How to Work Less and Enjoy Life More

The Perfect Interview: How to Get the Job You Really Want

Performance Appraisal: One More Time

The Effective Interviewer

Interviewing for Managers: A Complete Guide to Employment Interviewing

The New Cook's Cookbook (With Sebastian Milardo)

Finding a Job When Jobs Are Hard to Find (With Jurg Oppliger)

Booklets

A CEO's Guide to Interpersonal Relations

Counseling Techniques for the Non-Personnel Executive

The Complete Guide to Campus Interviewing

The Exit Interview

The Panel Interview

The Campus Interview

How to Drop Five Strokes without Having One

Finding More Enjoyment in Senior Golf

John D. Drake, PhD

A senior himself

OPEN BOOK
EDITIONS
A Berrett-Koehler Partner

How to Drop Five Strokes without Having One
Finding More Enjoyment in Senior Golf

iUniverse books may be ordered through booksellers or by contacting:

iUniverse
1663 Liberty Drive
Bloomington, IN 47403
www.iuniverse.com
1-800-Authors (1-800-288-4677)

ISBN: 978-1-4620-6038-2 (sc)
ISBN: 978-1-4620-6037-5 (hc)
ISBN: 978-1-4620-6039-9 (e)

Library of Congress Control Number: 2011918449

Printed in the United States of America

iUniverse rev. date: 11/10/2011

For PGA golf professionals

In appreciation for helping me, and countless others,
not only to learn the game but, more importantly, to enjoy it.

Contents

Contents

Preface

Seniors Helping Seniors

Clearly, my name isn't Hogan, Palmer, Woods, or Mickelson. I'm not even a golf professional. How could a book by some amateur—an aging senior, no less—be helpful in lowering your golf scores?

The answer is simple. I've been where you are. As a senior golfer I've seen my play gradually change both physically and mentally—my drive is shorter, but, on the plus side, poor shots don't unglue me as they used to. I've learned that I can still improve my game, despite my eighty years. In fact, during the past year my handicap dropped six strokes, and I won both our club's member-guest and member-member tournaments. My goal is to help you achieve similar success and to increase your enjoyment in playing.

How did I do it? Well, first of all, I experimented with alternative shots and strategies to compensate for my aging. A positive by-product of this experimentation was that I discovered a few unique and sometimes unconventional ways to the cup. I wasn't certain which of these findings would work best for other seniors, so I decided to put my findings to the test. For example, for the shots presented in this book, I hit twenty-five balls the conventional way and twenty-five using one of my senior alternatives. I tallied the differences, and the options that proved to be most productive are described here for you.

Do yips sometimes mess up your putts? Do first tee tensions result in embarrassing worm-burners? If your answer is yes to either of these questions, my psychological insights (I'm a "shrink") will help you conquer your feelings of anxiety and pressure. Golf should be fun; this book is dedicated to helping you experience more of it.

The suggestions presented here are easy to implement—you don't have to learn a new system or swing. In fact, the book contains hardly anything about "the swing." Instead, you will find specific techniques and strategies that you can readily adapt to your own swing—any one of which could cut strokes off your scorecard.

Here's an example:

Sharon, the wife of one of my senior golfing partners, tried one of my suggested alternative strategies—the flat take-back bump-and-run (chapter 4). She had been using her pitching and sand wedge to lob onto the green, but now (except for certain situations) Sharon uses the senior-tested bump-and-run. She dropped, on average, four strokes per round and is amazed at how more often she ends up close to the pin.

Some shots and strategies offered in this book run counter to what's currently in vogue. That's okay, because some of the ways we're taught to play are difficult for our older bodies to implement. In *How to Drop Five Strokes* you'll discover some easy-to-use options designed for bodies that won't allow us to swing the club as we once did.

Also, you can focus on only those parts of the game that give you trouble. If one recommended idea works for you, great; look through the book for another, and watch your scores go down.

Another reason this book may help your game is that the instructions are simple and are made even easier by use of many photographs. You will quickly note, from some photos, that I play left-handed. Lefties will like that, and right-handers tell me that with the arrow (in the photos) pointing toward the target, it's relatively easy to transpose photos for righty use. To help further, more than half the photos portray a right-handed player.

What about consulting a golf professional? Please do. Anyone who is serious about golf, regardless of age, can benefit from expert direction on developing a swing appropriate for his or her physical condition and skills. This book is neither designed to teach a swing nor to replace a professional's guidance. In fact, you'll find it helpful to take this book to a golf pro and ask him/her to help you implement shots you would like to use.

My fondest wish is that *How to Drop Five Strokes* will help senior golfers rejuvenate their game and experience more fun on the course.

John D. Drake
Tequesta, Florida

Acknowledgments

I would like to express my appreciation to all those who so willingly gave their time to this book. My gratitude to:

- Paul Compare, whose patience and skill produced all the photographs.

- Jack Kelly, Dick Lamberts, Rob Drake, Sebastian Milardo, Herman Krone, Ken Sheeleigh, Jo Ann Drake, Bob Bye, Gus Wilson, Len and Muriel Franceschini, and Lou Bragaw, whose suggestions helped shape this book.

- Val Marier and Bob Herzig, whose constructive critiques improved the book's clarity and accuracy.

- Fritz and BJ Clarke, Ann Barnes, Dee Drake—golfers who posed for the photos having to demonstrate the author's way and not their own excellent swings.

- The golf professionals who have helped me learn to play and develop my enjoyment of the game: Ken Raynor, Sam Marzenell, Bill Brown, Christopher Hayes, and Mark Mahon. Ken, Sam, and Chris also provided invaluable feedback about ways in which the book can help improve the play of seniors.

- My loving wife, Delia, who, after seven books, once again read every word and provided countless constructive suggestions.

My heartfelt thanks to you all.

Chapter 1

The Senior Game

> Golfer: "Do you think I can get there with a 5-iron?"
> Caddy: "Eventually."

"Ten years ago I could easily have cleared that pond."

"I'm okay until about the fourteenth hole, then I can feel myself getting tired."

"I've had to shorten my backswing, otherwise my old back will keep me up all night."

Sound familiar?

As much as we may hate to admit it, at sixty-plus we're different. We're different from younger golfers both physically and mentally. These changes usually come slowly and subtly. While not necessarily bad, they do impact how we play. The good news is that awareness of these changes allows us to adapt to them; we can still lower our scores and get more fun from our favorite pastime.

"More fun" and "lower scores" aren't just wishful thinking. This is a special time in most of our lives—the pressure of earning a living is gone or reduced, our families are raised, and, finally, we have time to relax with the game. We can approach the game with a new perspective—one that leads to making golf more satisfying than ever before. *How to Drop Five Strokes* is your guidebook to that enjoyment.

Younger versus Older—How We're Different

Physically: Clearly, our game is not the same as when we were thirty-five or forty. We're not, for example, as physically strong or as flexible. Perhaps we can't drive the ball as far as we used to, and we may not walk the course anymore. But there are adjustments we can make (described in the following chapters) that will enable us to perform quite well, despite our aging bodies.

Mentally: For most of us, the biggest after-sixty change is our attitude or mental set, a shift that is usually subtle and gradual.

One common attitude shift is a growing awareness of our limitations. We know that we're not going to drop ten strokes off our handicap. We don't seem to have the internal drive to take endless lessons and/or to consistently practice. Instead, we come to accept that the scores we're posting now are a little higher than they used to be. We may want them to be substantially lower, but we can live with the thought that it's not likely to happen.

Bill C., seventy-three, put it this way:

"What's different (from when I was younger)? That's easy. I'm more relaxed. If I have a bad hole, it doesn't 'throw me' anywhere near as much as it used to."

Senior golfer Eleanor T. told me:

"I just thank God I'm out here walking around and still able to play. When I was younger my score seemed to be the most important thing. Don't get me wrong, I still like to get a good score, but if I don't, so what?"

Another attitude change has to do with competitiveness. Of course we still want to win the match; that will never change. But for most of us, the intensity is less. We can lose more gracefully. We are inclined to adopt a "win a few; lose a few" mentality. And that's good. It doesn't raise our blood pressure, and we end up being more fun to play with.

Finally, as seniors, we don't have to prove anything to others or ourselves. We can more easily be our own person—we can quit after fifteen holes if we're too fatigued; we can more comfortably cancel a match if the weather isn't good, or we can do whatever makes the game more fun to play (such as taking an occasional mulligan).

All the aforementioned senior mentalities set the stage for a changed game—one that can optimize your enjoyment. To get you started on that road, I've listed below some specific suggestions for wringing more pleasure from your senior golf.

Quick Review

The Senior Game versus Younger Years

- **Physically we are less flexible**
- **Mentally we can more easily accept a bad shot**

Suggestions for More Enjoyment

- Play with companions you enjoy being with. Friendly rounds help you relax during play and can lead to a good time after the round.

- Take pleasure in small achievements. Maybe you didn't have a particularly good score, but your chipping was outstanding. Dwell on those good shots, and let them bring a smile to your face.

- Don't wear yourself out. Use a cart more often. If you now walk the eighteen, try walking nine and riding nine.

- Have one of your partners keep score. Don't ask about or pay attention to each score per hole. Rather, play each hole simply for the fun of conquering it. If you've never done this, try it; you'll be amazed at how many self-induced pressures vanish.

- Use dependable clubs. For example, if you have a favorite hybrid club, use it on the fairways even though you can sometimes hit the ball farther with other fairway woods or metals. Good, solid hits bring a sense of quiet satisfaction.

- Plan to reach the greens in regulation plus one stroke. This strategy reduces the pressure to hit long drives and fairway shots. Using higher numbered clubs may also result in greater accuracy, enabling you to avoid hazards. Who doesn't like that?

- Set realistic expectations for your performance. Don't expect perfection—there is no such thing in golf. If you typically screw up four holes a round, let that be your expectation so that when you have a poor hole, you simply chalk it up to "one of the bad ones" and continue to play without upset and tension.

- Play games. Games such as "six, six, six" and others can add fun to the round, just so long as the stakes are low. See chapter 9, "Games That Seniors Play," for a list of possibilities.

In the chapters ahead, we'll explore in more depth some easy ways to implement these enjoyment-producing ideas.

Quick Review

Suggestions for More Enjoyment

- **Play with friends**
- **Relish small successes**
- **Ride cart more often**
- **Don't keep your own score**
- **Use dependable clubs**
- **Go for greens in regulation + one**
- **Set realistic expectations**
- **Play golf games**

The Senior Game—Summary

Our age and years of living open the door to a new mentality about playing the game. As a result, senior golf can become the best of our golfing years. Happiness follows when you tee off with the goal of enjoying yourself and being thankful for the gift of health and the ability to play.

Chapter 2

On the Tee Box

It's better to be straight than long.

Is there any sound sweeter than that crisp "click" your driver makes as it crunches the ball? Add to that the ego-rewarding experience of seeing your ball sail high and straight down the fairway. No wonder we get addicted to golf.

While the psychic rewards of a good drive are many, so are the consequences of a poor one. A badly hit ball off the first tee, for instance, often sets the stage for screwing up the next few shots. For most of us, success on the tee box is vital for our enjoyment of a round.

In this chapter, we'll discuss how seniors can become more comfortable on the tee box, increase the likelihood of hitting longer well-placed drives, and get to the hole in fewer strokes. Sound good? Let's begin.

Managing Tee Box Stress

We all want to perform well, especially in front of our golfing companions. It's this desire to look good that often generates tension at a time when it's most important to be loose. And, of course, our looseness depends upon how confident we feel. When it's time to tee up, here are four ways to increase that confidence and to minimize tension.

1. Complete a preshot routine.

Using an established routine feels comfortable; it can be reassuring and it establishes a rhythm. If you don't already have such a routine, try one out. It could be a helpful addition to your game. Here's a typical preshot routine:

- Stand a few paces behind the ball and determine your target.
- Lock the target image in your mind.
- Pick a spot on the ground (four to five feet in front of the tee box) that is on your target line. I call it my "lineup" spot.
- Take a practice swing away from the ball. (Try to have a purpose to this swing. For example, "I'm going to try to keep my head behind the ball even as I begin my follow-through.)
- Step up, address the ball, and align your clubface perpendicular to your "lineup" spot.

Take the time to perform each step the same way every time you tee up. Unconsciously, your body will be getting acclimated and ready for the swing that is to follow. You might also silently say to yourself, "Okay, here we go—just another routine shot."

2. Use a self-talk swing reminder.

Let's say that you've completed your preshot routine and are now addressing the ball. A second way to distract yourself from tee box pressures is to make use of a simple swing thought—one that you use on every tee box as you begin your backswing. Here's one that Johnny Miller mentioned on the air: As he takes his driver back, he says to himself, slowly and rhythmically, "*John ... ny*" and as he starts his downswing, he says, "*Mil ... ler*" with the same pace and cadence as on his backswing.

Bob Bye, a senior friend of mine, uses this one: He refers to it as his three *s*'s, namely, "sweep, shift, swing." He says his first *s* as he begins his take-back (wanting to keep the initial part of his backswing close to the ground). On the next *s* he shifts his weight to his front foot, and for the last *s* he makes his swing.

My swing talk is: "*sl ... ow*" (backswing) "*mo ... tion*" (downswing). This swing talk focuses my attention and takes my mind off thinking about swing mechanics and the people around me. It also helps me slow down, a problem I struggle with.

3. Use a dependable club.

This may mean foregoing your driver if you are more confident with your 3-wood, 5-wood, hybrid, or even your 6-iron. Unless you usually can get on the green in regulation, it won't matter too much how far that first shot travels, but it will matter if you end up in the rough.

4. Loosen your hands and forearms.

For most of us seniors, it now takes longer to get loose than when we were younger. So, before it's your group's turn to hit, and when no one is teeing off, stand off the tee box and take some practice swings that exaggerate being *slow* and *relaxed.* Make sure you are holding the club with your fingers and not your palm. You'll know when you're "loose" if your fingers can gently jiggle the club.

It's also beneficial, between swings, to let your arms dangle at your sides and gently shake them.

Quick Review

Managing Tee Box Stress

- **Follow a preshot routine**
- **Use a self-talk swing reminder**
- **Use a dependable club**
- **Loosen hands and forearms**

Tee Box Smarts—Adding to Your Pleasure

In this section we'll discuss two tee box strategies for getting more enjoyment from your game along with the bonus of lowering your scores.

1. Move up to a forward tee box.

The idea is to move forward to a tee box from which you can reach most of the greens in regulation. I have yet to talk with a senior who has "moved up" that hasn't found more satisfaction from his/her day on the course. Playing the forward tees often takes hazards out of play, and the shorter distances enable you to swing more easily. The result: good feelings about yourself and lower scores.

Put aside your ego. For most of us, the major obstacle to moving forward is our ego. It's hard to accept that we're not as powerful as we used to be—that we're not playing from the same tees as the younger players. My golf partner, Gordon Grant, dealt with the self-image problem in this way. He said,

> *"I've moved up because I'm old and can't drive really long ones. After only two rounds from the forward tees I saw how much more satisfying a round could be—especially on the par 5s. So, I said to myself, 'I've earned this privilege.' Hey, I'm still playing golf and that's a lot more than some guys younger than me can say."*

2. Don't plan to reach greens in regulation.

On par 4s and par 5s, what percent of the time do you make the greens in regulation? If your answer is "less than half the time," you're not alone; most seniors are rarely on the green in regulation. Nonetheless, we strive for distance off the tee box and work hard at getting a long second shot. The problem is that, in the trying, we often miss-hit. We press to accomplish more than our bodies will allow, often resulting in disappointing results.

Senior strategy

Plan to reach the green in regulation *plus one stroke*. Yes, you read that right; on most holes we're not going to try to reach the par 4s in two and the par 5s in three. Instead, we're going to lower our scores by playing "smart golf."

3. Play smart golf.

Smart golf has to do with making distances work for us. Let's use par 4's as an example. For men, the average par 4 (middle tee box) is about 360 yards. If you employ our sixty-plus strategy (planning to reach the green in three shots), each shot only needs to be 120 yards! But wait, it gets better. Assume you can hit your tee shot 150 yards. That leaves only 210 yards—two iron shots of about 105 yards each. For most seniors, these distances can be attained relatively easily using a 7-, 8-, or 9-iron.

To make reaching the green even easier, suppose you don't use an iron for your first fairway shot but instead use your dependable hybrid or lofted fairway metal—a club you can easily hit about 130 yards. Now, for your third shot, you have only eighty yards to the green, a relatively easy distance for most of us.

For women, the average par 4 is 306 yards. Thus, getting to the green in three means three shots of about 102 yards. If you can drive 130 yards off the tee box, you only have to hit the next two shots eighty-eight yards. The "smart golf" strategy works as well for women as it does for men.

Even though your club choices and hitting distances may vary from those listed in the examples, the concept of taking three easy shots, as opposed to two long hits, will minimize miss-hits and help lower your scores.

Consider this about the strategy: If you are consistently on the green in regulation plus one, averaging two putts, you can bogie every hole. Most seniors would love to shoot bogie golf. On par 72 courses, it means you'll shoot a 90!

Some seniors may not be able to reach the green in one plus regulation. No problem. In these situations your plan is to reach the green in two plus regulation. The benefit is that you'll experience more enjoyment from the game because you are more consistently on the fairway and hitting solid shots (the result from using "easy" clubs and not pushing yourself). It's like the experience of ending up with a score that isn't great, but yet coming away with the feeling that you played quite well (except for a hole or two). When that happens, you feel good about the round, and isn't that what it's all about?

Why It Works

The reason senior, smart-golf strategy works is simple: it takes the pressure off. It allows you to use clubs—off the tee and on the fairway—that engender confidence. The result is that you are more relaxed, and you become a better ball-striker. Try this strategy for a few rounds, and the bet is that you'll enjoy the game more and end up with lower-than-usual scores.

Quick Review

Having More Fun off the Tee Box

- **Play from forward tees**
- **Play "smart golf"—greens in regulation plus one**

Senior Tee Box Strategies

1. Tee placement

This is a simple idea, but it has saved many a senior from getting into trouble. When facing a left- or right-hand hazard, place your tee on the same side of the tee box as is the hazard. For example, if a water hazard lines the left side of the fairway, tee off from the left side of the tee box. This strategy enables you to aim (and hit) diagonally away from potential problems (see Photo 2 A).

Photo 2 A

2. Tee box markers

Have you noticed that the tee box markers are sometimes placed at an unusual angle? That is, an imaginary line between the two markers is often not perpendicular to the middle of the fairway. Instead, the line is angled so that it lures you to line up so that you're aiming to the left or right side of the fairway. Do you suppose that groundskeepers purposely do that just to throw us off?

In any case, as you set up for your drive, ignore the direction the tee box markers suggest, and align yourself with your fairway target. As was mentioned earlier, use of a "lineup" spot can aid in driving accuracy.

3. Level ground

Any sloping surface reduces the likelihood of a clean hit. Select the flattest area on the tee box, even if you have to move your tee back a few feet from the markers (but no more than two club lengths).

4. Reward versus risk in target selection

This chapter advocates a conservative tee shot, but it doesn't mean that, once in a while, you shouldn't "go for it." If there's a wide-open fairway in front of you, the risks for striving for distance are low.

Let's suppose a brook traverses the fairway at a distance close enough for you to hit over, but only if you hit a really good drive. Clearly there is risk here, so the question becomes, "Are the rewards worth it?" If getting over the brook only gains twenty or so yards, it might be better to lay up. On the other hand, if being over the brook places you, for example, in a good position to manage a dogleg, the gain is probably worth the risk.

If you are at all nervous about making it over the hazard, the odds favor laying up, regardless of the advantage of a long drive.

In almost all cases, don't take the risk unless the gain will result in one or two fewer strokes to the cup.

Quick Review

Senior's Tee Box Strategies

- **When a left or right fairway hazard exists, tee on the same side of the tee box as the hazard**
- **Don't be fooled by off-centered tee box markers**
- **Tee off from box's flattest space**
- **Consider gain versus risk in target selection**

Getting More Distance

1. Strive for a smooth, slow tempo.

As you no doubt have experienced, well-struck tee shots usually result from swings that are unhurried. Unfortunately, that's often difficult to achieve on the tee box because we're so tempted to get all we can out of our drive. In the effort to get distance, we let our arms take over; we swing them so fast that they get ahead of our body rotation, usually resulting in a slice, hook, or topped ball. Here are two ways to help slow down our arms:

a. **Use a one-piece take-back.** The "one-piece" refers to a backswing in which your shoulders and arms turn as one unit. You let your shoulders bring the club back, not your arms. This action automatically shifts your weight to your back foot and sets the stage for a downswing led by your body's counter rotation. This results in a powerful swing. Anne S., a senior golfer friend, says this about her use of the one-piece take-back:

    "It seems as though I'm hardly swinging, but I'm always amazed at how far the ball travels."

    A key to the successful use of this take-back is keeping your forward arm as straight as possible.

b. **Take a few practice swings with your driver's head cover on.** The cover's resistance to the air slows up the action, providing a good feel of your body turn controlling the swing and your arms swinging slowly.

2. Extend your arms.

Want more distance? Without adding muscle, seniors can get it by swinging their clubhead in a wider arc. It starts with your backswing. As you bring the club back, extend your left arm (right-handers) as far to the right as you can. When I take my backswing, it feels as though my shoulder is pushing my arm away from my body. This action results in a straighter lead arm, which, in turn, creates a wider arc. The wider arc produces increased centrifugal force and clubhead speed. You'll be surprised how this simple action, coupled with the one-piece take-back, adds significant distance to your drive.

Photo 2 B shows this arm extension at the beginning of a backswing.

Photo 2 B

3. Driver and ball selection.

Senior men and women can increase their driving distance by using a light driver. Reduced club weight makes it easier and less tiring to swing, which in turn, results in faster clubhead speed. I recently switched to a lighter driver and added ten or more yards to each drive. Drivers with flexible shafts can also help with distance. It can be helpful to see a pro about a "fitting." He or she can determine the best length, weight, and flex for your new driver, depending upon your body size and swing speed.

Using low-compression balls can also attain greater distance.

Quick Review

Getting More Distance

- **Use a one-piece take-back**
- **Take practice swings designed to slow swing speed**
- **Extend you arms**
- **Use lightweight driver and low-compression balls**

On the Tee Box—Summary

- It's better to be straight than long.
- Reduce tee box tension by:
    1. Implementing a consistent preshot routine
    2. Using self-talk reminders
    3. Selecting your most dependable club
    4. Loosening your hands and forearms

- Play "smart golf." On most par 4's and par 5's, plan to reach the green in one stroke over regulation or play from a forward tee box.

- Place your tee on the same side of the tee box as is a hazard.

- Seek a level spot on which to place your tee.

- Consider risk versus reward on potentially dangerous tee shots.

- Strive to swing your driver with a slow, even tempo.

- Widen your swing arc.

- Use a one-piece take-back.

- Use a lightweight driver and low-compression balls.

Chapter 3

On the Fairway

> Drives that end up in the middle of
> the fairway almost always produce
> a quiet, inner satisfaction.

Conquering that piece of real estate between your ball and the green can be frustrating; bunkers, rough, and all kinds of hazards may come into play. So, in this chapter, we'll look at seven common fairway problems and some senior alternatives for getting to the green.

Problem #1—Second Shot on Par 4's and Par 5's

I remember reading somewhere that the hardest club to use is the 3-wood. Whether that's true or not, I'm uncertain, but it can often be an exasperating club. If I'm going to slice a shot, it is most likely to occur with my 3-wood. I probably rush the shot or swing too fast because I am striving for distance.

Many seniors experience the same kind of difficulty with their 2-, 3-, or 4-irons.

Senior strategy

As we discussed in chapter 2, seniors can lower their scores by using fairway clubs that work most consistently rather than those that can be hit longer. We talked about the value of making your goal that of being on the green in regulation *plus one*. For example, I prefer my 5-wood to my 3-wood; it usually flies straight and carries almost as far. Many of my senior friends prefer to use a favorite hybrid club.

The suggested alternative embodies the concept of percentages. You play those clubs whose odds favor your getting sufficiently near the green so that you have a relatively easy third shot (par 4s). Hit your next shot close to the pin, and you can still make par!

Problem #2—"In Between Clubs" for Shots to the Green

I hate having to hit to the green when my lie is "between clubs." For me, it often means that I'm too close to use my pitching wedge, but too far for my sand wedge. In these instances, I have to make a "feel shot." I can't take a full swing (pitching wedge), and my half or three-quarter attempt often results in a shot that is too short or too long.

Senior strategy

One option is to purchase a gap wedge with a loft that falls between the pitching wedge and sand wedge.

If you're not interested in adding another club to your bag, a second option is to avoid a lob shot altogether. I have discovered that when I'm in between clubs, and I have between fifty to one hundred yards to the pin, hitting a midiron on a relatively flat trajectory usually gets me close to the pin. I see this shot as a modified bump and run—the ball being airborne about two-thirds of the way. Its use eliminates much of the risk involved in trying to reduce the carry of my pitching wedge or trying to get extra distance from the sand wedge.

After much experimentation, I found the 7-iron to be optimal for this shot. I cock my wrists, take a relatively low, straight backswing to about waist high, and then make a relaxed, straight downswing. The follow-through need be no more than waist height but should point right at the target. Use your front arm (left hand for right-handers) to guide your direction. It's almost like an elongated putting stroke.

With a little practice, you will find this to be an easy shot. I have found that it practically eliminates the likelihood of the ball being hit too far left or right of your target. That advantage itself will help lower your scores.

Problem #3—Fairway Bunkers

If you land in a fairway bunker, undoubtedly you "ripped" your drive. The downside is that you have a more difficult second shot and often good course management dictates that you hit your normal bunker shot, simply to get the ball back on the fairway.

On the other hand, you may want to try to advance the ball to the green. To help you with this decision, we'll look at two relatively long bunker shots—one requiring fifty to one hundred yards and another one-hundred-plus yards.

Senior strategy

1. Fifty to One Hundred Yards: With the green this close, a shot to the flag is possible, but it requires picking the ball cleanly off the sand. Not easy to do. To succeed with this shot, I have discovered that it is essential to prevent my front foot from sliding forward on the downswing. Unless I have that foot securely anchored (dug down until it rests on the hard ground) I am likely to hit the sand behind the ball and mess up the shot. Setting up with the ball farther back in your stance than normal will also help to avoid striking the sand first.

Most seniors can use their irons for this shot, selecting one club more than you would normally use for the distance involved. Also, bend your knees more than usual to compensate for the inches you've dug into the sand. It is helpful to minimize lower body motion so that your feet can provide a stable platform.

2. One Hundred Yards or More: If the bunker has a low lip between your ball and the direction of the green, consider using a 5-wood, 7-wood, or hybrid club.

Establish a firm platform for your feet, choke down, take a relatively flat backswing, swing smoothly at the ball, and follow through. You want to make contact with the ball *before* hitting the sand.

Use of flat-bottomed woods or metals will advance the ball a long way toward the green and, more importantly, will take much of the risk out of the bunker shot. Even if you strike the sand behind the ball, the club's flat bottom will allow the club to slide along the sand and firmly contact the ball.

If the bunker has a medium-high lip (in front of you) consider the use of a higher wood (7, 9) or utility club.

Problem #4—Swing Hampered by an Obstacle

Your shot ends up near a tree or some obstacle so that you can't take a full swing without your club hitting it. Photo 3 A shows a commonly encountered situation.

Photo 3 A

27

Senior strategy
Shorten the club length to accommodate the space available. By selecting a short club, such as your pitching wedge and by choking down, you may have room to make at least a small swing.

If swinging your arms becomes almost impossible, try separating your hands on the club (see Photo 3 B) to get sufficient leverage.

Photo 3 B

In most cases, simply try to hit the ball to where you can take a normal swing, rather than attempting to substantially advance it.

If no swing seems feasible, forget about all the miraculous recoveries you've seen Tiger and Phil make. For us seniors, the odds favor declaring your ball an "unplayable lie" and taking a one-stroke penalty. Remember, you can decide to take such a lie at any time, except in a water hazard.

Since we've just mentioned "unplayable lie," this might be a good time to review that rule. Here are your options. For a one-stroke penalty you may:

- Return to the spot from which you hit the ball and hit again.
- Drop your ball within two club lengths from where it lies, but not nearer the hole.
- Drop your ball at any point behind where your ball lay, keeping it on a line directly between the hole and the spot on which you drop your ball.

Problem #5—Hillside or Uneven Lies

Balls that are not resting on a flat spot can often result in disappointing hits. Here's a quick review of ways that will help you make solid contact with the ball when the surface is irregular.

Senior strategy
If the ball lies:
- *Above your feet:* Choke down on your club.
- *Below your feet:* Stand closer to the ball than usual and bend your knees sufficiently so that the clubhead can touch the ground behind the ball.

- *On uphill slope:* Keep shoulders parallel to the angle of the slope. Position the ball a little forward in your stance, and take a flat backswing (to avoid hitting the ground behind the ball). Since the ball is likely to have a higher-than-usual trajectory, take one more lower-lofted club than normal.
- *On downhill slope:* Keep shoulders parallel to the slope. Position the ball farther back in your stance. To minimize topping the ball, accentuate a follow-through that matches the contour of the slope.

Problem #6—In the Rough

It always amazes me to see the pros hit long distances from high rough, going for a green that's a couple of hundred yards away. However, it has been my experience that most senior players lack the physical strength to succeed at such shots.

Senior strategy
When the rough is not very high—six inches or less—and the grass/weeds are bent toward your target, seniors can usually advance the ball a fair distance using a hybrid club or an iron. I have found that these shots (grass bent toward the target) often "fly" (i.e., when they land, they roll farther than usual). So, if you are within range of the green, use a higher-lofted club than when hitting from the fairway. When the grass is higher than six inches, wet, or bent away from the target, the best senior strategy is to simply get the ball out onto the fairway and not concern yourself with distance.

One option is to try a wedge. It's the heaviest club in your bag, and this weight is helpful. Come down steeply on the ball to hit it up and out of the rough. Don't try to "muscle" the ball out with your arms, but instead firmly grip your club and bring your club around with a strong body turn. These actions will help to counteract the grass's resistance. Opening your clubface a bit will help compensate for the clubhead becoming closed as the grass wraps around the shaft's hosel. When the grass is wet, this "wrapping around" problem is magnified.

In situations in which you believe that you will be unable to apply enough power to extricate your ball—for me, rough that is six inches or higher—the odds favor taking an unplayable lie. Finding a more suitable spot for hitting is just good course management as opposed to vainly taking a few shots to clear the rough.

Problem #7—Drainage Ditch

On a course where I often play, several fairways are edged with drainage ditches. They can be a pain to get out of. The problem is to get down to the ball in a way that enables you to make a reasonably good swing.

Senior strategy
You can succeed in extricating yourself from such hazards by substantially bending at the waist. Spreading your legs wider than usual also brings you closer to the ball. These actions will help you to get your club to the ball without being bunched up by exaggerated knee bend.

On the Fairway—Summary

- On fairways, use clubs that you can usually hit well. Most seniors will end up with better scores by placing their priority on keeping the ball on the fairway as opposed to risking hazards by going for distance.

- Instead of trying to get as close to the green as possible, try to place your second shot on par 4s or third shot on par 5s, at a spot that enables you to take a full, normal swing for your shot onto the green.

- When one hundred yards or less from the pin, and you are between clubs, consider hitting a 7-iron bump-and-run rather than modifying your usual swing with your pitching wedge or sand wedge.

- When in fairway bunkers, consider using a lofted fairway wood for one-hundred-plus yards. For forty to sixty yards, use midiron with standard sand swing.

- On hillside lies, focus on keeping your shoulders parallel with the slope.

- When in high rough, make your goal one of simply getting your ball out onto the fairway rather than muscling it out for distance.

Chapter 4

Around the Green

A chip-in = instant exuberance

Reducing your putts is the best single way to reduce your score.

Clearly, the closer you land to the pin, the more often you'll one- or two-putt. So let's start there. How do you chip close most of the time? This chapter explores the possibilities.

Some seniors have trouble chipping/pitching accurately. Too bad, because it is one aspect of the game that doesn't require a lot of strength or flexibility—it's these shots that can help us seniors avoid an escalating handicap.

For quite awhile, I was so bad at approach-to-the-green shots that I was compelled to find a better way. And, I did. I developed several effective ways to chip or pitch, the choice depending upon the terrain confronting me and the distance to the green. Here are three common situations that golfers encounter, along with some senior-tested strategies for coping with them:

- Fifty yards or less from the green, path is open
- Fifty yards or less from the green, path is blocked
- One to five yards off the green, on the fairway

Situation #1—Fifty Yards or Less from Green, Path Is Open

The setting

Between you and the green there may be some fairway undulations, the green may be slightly raised, and perhaps bunkers guard both sides—something like the scene in Photo 4 A. But, all in all, there is a relatively smooth, open pathway.

Photo 4 A

What's Best—Lob or Bump?

Conventional way

With fifty yards or less to the green, many of my golfer friends—and most golf books—recommend hitting a high lob. They say that with such a shot the ball is likely to land softly and stay on the green, and that if you bump and run, there is too much chance for the ball to bounce off the desired path.

Senior strategy

My research has shown that seniors will more consistently get close to the pin with a *bump-and-run* than with a high lob.

For most high-handicappers, distance control is difficult with relatively short, highly lofted shots. In the situation being discussed, fifty yards or less from the pin, poor shots often stem from not having the right wedge so that you can take a full swing. Instead, you are faced with a half or three-quarter swing that requires careful judgment.

Test results

I put the lob versus bump concept to the test. One day I placed myself fifty yards from the pin. I alternately lobbed twenty-five shots with my sand wedge and bumped twenty-five with my 9-iron. Only ten of the lobs ended up within five feet of the pin, but nineteen of the bumps fell within that circle! That was pretty convincing.

Of course, you may be more skillful at using your highly lofted clubs so that my findings aren't relevant for you. But even if you are good at lobbing, you might want to try senior-style bumping to see if you can do even better.

Succeeding with the Bump and Run—Senior Style

Seniors will do best with the bump-and-run when they:

1. Use the same club most of the time
2. Determine the best spot to land the ball
3. Take relatively straight backswing, keeping hands below the waist
4. Exaggerate the follow-through (toward the target)

Here's some detail on these four factors.

The club selection
Use a club that works well for you. Most likely, you already have a favorite. For most fifty-yard or less bump-and-runs, I use the 9-iron. It has reasonable loft, and yet is easy to control. Other golfers may prefer the 7- or 8-iron or the pitching wedge.

A key point for seniors: Whatever club you select, use the *same* club for most of your bump-and-runs—you'll begin to acquire a feel for how hard to strike the ball for various distances.

The landing area
Ideally, you want your bump-and-run shots to land on the fairway, near the green. This recommendation is contradicted by conventional theory which says that dropping the ball anyplace but on the green, or first cut, is too risky—that fairway undulations could bounce your ball in directions you won't like.

However, with the low-trajectory senior bump-and-run—especially from forty yards or more—it is unlikely you'll be able to fly the ball to the green and have it remain there. So, instead, you select a spot on the fairway that sufficiently slows the ball so that it rolls gently onto the green and near to the pin. Often this spot can be the sloped area that surrounds most raised greens. In Photo 4 B the darker shade of grass abutting the green surface reveals a significant upward slope.

Photo 4 B

As seniors, we should be willing to risk the occasional bad bounce (from landing on the fairway) because more often than not our bump-and-run pitch will bring us closer to the hole than a lob.

The swing

Conventional way
In most golf publications, pictures illustrating the correct pitch shot show the club shaft pointing skyward and the wrists cocked. Of course, on shots over sixty yards a bigger backswing and

wrist action will help you reach the green. However, on shots of fifty yards or less—the kind that we're discussing here—we are recommending the strategy as described below.

Senior strategy

Take a stance with your feet fairly close together and pointed slightly toward the target. Hands are placed slightly forward of the clubhead and the ball is near the back of your stance. In Photo 4 C, note that Fritz's knees are flexed and that his weight is slightly more on his front foot. Elbows should remain close to the body.

Photo 4 C

Take the club straight back along the target line. Extend both arms fully, but with *no wrist hinge.*

Your take-back distance depends upon how far the ball must travel. As the distance increases, the backswing becomes longer, but in no case should it be more than waist high (see Photo 4 D). This represents a major difference between the conventional and the senior shot. The low, straight backswing and fixed wrists reduce the possibilities for error, thus increasing accuracy and consistency. If you try this shot, it would be helpful to have someone check to see if your swing matches the photo.

If you experience any difficulty in making this shot, it is likely that your head has moved forward on the downswing. On a practice range, try concentrating on keeping your head still and over the ball until the clubhead is well out in front of you. A little practice time is worth it because this shot has great potential for reducing your scores.

Photo 4 D

On the downswing, rotate smoothly, coming slightly down on the ball. Your upper body (shoulders and arms) should bring the club forward, rather than your wrists. The key to success with this shot is *follow-through.* Don't stop the club after the ball is struck, but consciously let the clubhead rise toward the target (see Photo 4 E).

Photo 4 E

A good way to improve the accuracy of your bump-and-run is to identify a ground "marker"—a leaf, grass coloration, divot, or spot that is in a direct line between your ball and your target. Your aim is now established. As you take your practice swings, make certain that the clubhead is on line with your marker. Then, when you're ready to hit the ball, refocus on the target in order to judge the distance and the force needed to reach the cup.

Quick Review

Getting to the cup—Fifty yards or less from the green (open pathway)

- Odds favor bump-and-run versus lob
- Use same club most of the time
- Use a low, straight backswing with no wrist cock
- Exaggerate your follow-through

Situation #2—Fifty Yards or Less from Green, Path Is Blocked

The setting

The space between your ball and the green contains problems—it's steeply sloped, has nasty rough or trees or a bunker (maybe even two!). Obviously, the bump-and-run is inappropriate. We need a lob that flies over the problem area and drops our ball on the green (see Photo 4 F).

Photo 4 F

What's the Best Lob?

Conventional way

The lob shot in this kind of situation, especially when it must carry thirty to fifty yards, is usually accomplished with a high-lofted wedge. The swing plane is fairly vertical so that you can strike down on the ball. The stroke also involves strong wrist action. Photo 4 G shows how the conventional swing looks at the top of the backswing.

Photo 4 G

Senior strategy—The "swish" shot

For the reasons already mentioned, many senior golfers have difficulty with the conventional lob shot. Here is a way to make such a shot easy and effective.

I refer to this senior alternative as my "swish" shot, so named because that's the sound it makes as the club swings through the grass. The swish is unorthodox—I doubt that you'll find it in any golf magazine or book. But, it does wonders for me; it has gotten me out of trouble spots that used to seem impossible.

Basically, the swish is similar to a bunker shot (i.e., the clubface travels *under* the ball and imparts a high trajectory and backspin). When the ball lands, it rolls very little.

This shot is easiest to hit when the ball is sitting up (firm grass or short rough) or rests on loose dirt. However, you can also successfully use the swish shot on closely mown fairways. It is my shot of choice unless the ball is resting on a hard surface, in which case I resort to the more conventional shot.

Club selection

The only club I have ever used for this shot is the sand wedge. If the distance seems too far for a sand wedge, a pitching wedge might work, but my preference for long distances (up to fifty yards) is still the sand wedge. I simply take a bigger backswing to help increase the clubhead speed.

The swish swing

My feet are slightly open and spaced about sixteen inches apart. Knees are significantly bent and my weight is about equal on each foot (see Photo 4 H).

Photo 4 H

The clubface is very open—almost flat—so that it can easily be slid *under* the ball (not down and through the ball).

Your backswing should be quite low (not above your shoulders). In Photo 4 I, note how my arms are parallel to the ground. Wrists are *not* cocked. The downswing starts with the forward rotational turn of your shoulders and upper body.

Photo 4 I

As you swing toward the ball, make sure that your palm (right hand for right-handers) is facing skyward. This will ensure that your clubface is open as it passes under the ball. Your hands are ahead of the clubhead. Let your hips rotate naturally through the shot.

The key to successful execution of the swish is keeping the club moving—parallel to the ground—well past the spot where the ball was located. Make no effort to come upward in the follow-through. The flat angle of the clubface will cause the ball to sharply rise without any particular effort on your part (see Photo 4 J).

Photo 4 J

Once you start using the swish, you'll discover that it doesn't require much power to produce a high arc. You'll need to experiment a bit to determine how hard to strike the ball for various distances. You can have fun with this shot. It will carry your ball safely over all kinds of hazards and land it softly on the green. Try it and amaze your golfer companions.

Senior psychology: A productive mind-set for this shot is to make your goal one of chipping it in.

Quick Review

Getting to the cup—fifty yards or less from the green (pathway blocked)

- **Requires a lob**
- **Use "swish" shot**
- **Very open clubface—slide club under ball**

Situation #3—On the Fairway, One to Five Yards off the Green

You are on the fairway, not on the green's first cut (see Photo 4 K).

Photo 4 K

What's Best—Putt or Chip?

Conventional way
When not on the green or the first cut, most golf texts recommend chipping over the fairway onto the green.

Senior strategy
My testing shows that it is almost always to your advantage to putt, except when the:

> 1. Grass blades are bent toward you (i.e., you're hitting into the grain)

2. Fairway grass is wet

3. Fairway has obvious, rough patches

When these conditions exist, the odds favor your chipping rather than putting.

Test results

In an experiment similar to the one conducted for the bump-and-run shot, I selected a fairway spot about three yards off the edge of the green with fifteen more yards on the green to the pin. The grass was dry, blades bent somewhat toward the green, and the fairway was reasonably smooth.

I alternated twenty fairway putts (with putter) and twenty chip shots (with a pitching wedge) from the same location. Seventeen of the putts stopped within three feet of the cup, but only thirteen of the chips came that close. A few weeks later, a senior female golfer repeated this test with similar results—actually, she had two more putts closer to the pin than I managed!

My golf buddies often questioned my putting from the fairway, but their comments ceased when they saw how close I usually got to the pin. Most seniors will also benefit by putting rather than by chipping. As the saying goes, "A bad putt is always better than a bad chip."

The swing

Use your usual putting swing, but since you must traverse some fairway grass, you'll be taking a slightly longer backswing (to generate sufficient clubhead momentum).

What's Best—Pin In or Out?

Senior strategy

When chipping or putting onto the green, the odds favor removing the pin. While I have no statistical data to offer, my thirty years of golfing experience has been that balls striking the pin usually ricochet away from the hole; rarely do they drop in. So, here's a guiding principle for seniors: *If you think there is a reasonable possibility the chip or putt could be holed, remove the pin.*

The exception is when the path to the hole is steeply downhill. In such cases, you're hoping the pin will stop a ball that might roll too far past the hole.

Quick Review

Getting to the Cup—One to five yards off the green (on fairway)

> - **Odds favor putting versus chipping**
> - **Remove pin from cup**

Around the Green—Summary

- The quickest way to reduce your score is to chip more effectively.

- Consider using the "swish" shot whenever you need to lob over a hazard.

- When one to five yards from the green, the odds favor putting rather than chipping.

- There is no one "chipping stroke." The swing and club you use depend upon the conditions between your ball and the pin.

- Determine the type of stroke you will consistently use in "around the green" situations. Three senior alternative shots are recommended for you to try out.

- Make dropping in the cup your chipping goal, not just to be on the green or close to the pin.

- If you think you have a reasonable chance to sink a putt or chip in, remove the pin.

- More than half of any practice time should be spent on your short game—shots of one hundred yards or less. Such effort will have more payoff than working on your drive and fairway woods.

Chapter 5

On the Beach (Greenside)

> Half of your problems with bunker shots will be cured by hitting through the sand without closing the clubface.

"Oh, no. Please don't go in there!" It's a plea often heard as a ball heads toward a bunker. But, dear readers, even though bunkers are designed to make the course more challenging, they needn't be a burden. In fact, there are many occasions when I would rather be in a bunker than, let's say, having to chip over it.

In this chapter, I'll share with you what I have learned about hitting out of the sand. If it works for me, it might do the same for you.

The setting
We're talking here about greenside bunkers with a run-of-the-mill lie. The ball isn't buried and it isn't stuck under a grass lip. In other words, it's a makeable chip. Balls that are resting under

the bunker's lip or half on the grass and half in the sand call for special techniques that are beyond the scope of this book. But, as an experienced senior golfer, I have found that the smartest strategy with these problem lies is to *get out of the bunker by hitting the ball in whatever direction you can—even if it means hitting it away from the green.*

The conventional bunker shot

Most books by professional golfers describe the greenside bunker shot as involving an open stance, early wrist cock, and a vertical swing plane. On the downswing, effort is made to hit down into the sand directly behind the ball. There are many variations on this theme, depending upon the condition of the sand (wet/dry) and the distance the ball must carry.

Senior bunker shot

At the risk of sounding immodest, my friends consider me to be a good bunker player. I've become reasonably good at coping with the sand because the course I play in Florida is loaded with greenside bunkers; I was simply forced to learn an effective way.

In the past, I experienced some difficulty with the expert's vertical swing path. Frequently, my clubhead went too deeply into the sand, and, consequently, the ball did not move out of the bunker or, worse yet, I struck the ball (I'm too embarrassed to describe the consequences!). I've found that to successfully execute the vertical sand shot swing, your arm and wrist action must be impeccable. No doubt, with training from a pro, and lots of practice, seniors can achieve success with the conventional bunker shot. In the meantime, I eliminate from my bunker play the two factors that mess up the average senior's sand shot—the vertical descent and the wrist action.

Nature of the shot
Basically, this bunker shot is like the "swish" shot (chapter 4). If you can do that shot, the bunker shot will be easy for you.

The swing
I almost always use my sand wedge in greenside bunkers. Even though it is a short club, I take a wide stance—about sixteen inches. This gives me a stable platform. It is essential that you be firmly anchored in the sand so that your feet won't slide with your downswing. Wiggle your shoes until you feel firm ground.

Stance. A slightly open one works best for me. The ball is near the middle of the stance or slightly rear of middle (see Photo 5 A). Notice, too, that BJ's knees are quite flexed. The flex helps her transfer her weight from back to front foot, and also helps to compensate for the distance her feet have dug into the sand. The clubface is very open (almost flat).

Photo 5 A

Backswing. It begins with the turning of your upper body. Your hips remain facing the ball and turn only slightly. Wrists are *not* cocked. The backswing is rather close to the sand—definitely not vertical. This is the senior difference; it's not the conventional sand shot. I recommend it to you because it works better than any other bunker shot I've tried.

Photo 5 B

Downswing. Start by focusing your eyes on a spot three to four inches behind the ball—that's where you want your clubface to contact the sand. The downswing travels along a flat plane so that the clubhead impacts the sand well behind the ball, shallowly digs into the sand (no deeper than an inch), slides under the ball, and lets the sand's pressure against the ball drive it out of the bunker. It usually comes out "soft" and with a nice backspin. A helpful visual guide to this swing is to imagine a business envelope lying on the sand with your ball in the center. As you swing forward, your club impacts the sand at one end of the envelope, travels under the ball, and emerges at the envelope's other end.

Clubface angle. When it is necessary to get the ball up very quickly (for example, when close to the lip of the bunker), the clubface is completely open—almost flat. For a high, arcing shot, it's also helpful to lower your hands (more knee and back bend).

When the ball must carry a long way, let's say twenty yards, slightly close the face to reduce the loft and produce more distance. The degree to which you close the face is a judgment that needs to be learned by experimentation. Not a big deal; a half hour in a practice bunker will give you a good feel for it—at least as a start.

Making the shot work.
There are two key actions for succeeding with this shot:

1. Keeping the clubface open as it travels beneath the ball and beyond it.
2. Accelerating the clubhead through the sand well into the follow-through. Don't stop the swing once the clubhead passes under the ball.

In general, bunker swings should be smooth and relaxed. Most of the time, you don't have to hit the sand with fast clubhead speed to get the ball up and out. It's helpful if you experience the feeling that your follow through is exaggerated.

This shot works so well that soon your expectation will be to chip it near or in the hole and not simply to get out of the bunker and onto the green.

Quick Review

Bunker Shot for Seniors

- Wide stance—dig feet into sand
- Low backswing, open clubface
- No wrist cock
- Flat downswing, wrists firm
- Slide club through the sand, starting three to four inches behind the ball
- Exaggerate the follow-through

Senior Psychology

You can't succeed with bunker shots if you are tentative. The swing needs to be made with the confidence that your ball will sail out of the sand and roll near the hole. One good way to achieve this confidence is to practice this simple swing. You'll find that it's easy to learn and, once you've got the feel for it, you won't worry a bit about your next bunker encounter. Your confidence will also be enhanced knowing that if you focus your eyes on a spot several inches behind the ball, it is unlikely that you will strike the ball first and thus send it flying across the green, and maybe into another bunker!

On the Beach—Summary

- Being "anchored" in the sand is important. Wiggle your shoes until you feel a solid base.

- The senior, no-wrist bunker shot described here makes it easy to keep your sand wedge flat and minimizes errors. Do not dig deeper than one inch.

- Successful greenside bunker shots require taking sand three to four inches behind the ball and having an extended follow-through.

- The distance the ball flies out of the bunker is a function of the openness of the clubface and your clubhead speed.

- For longer carry, slightly close the clubface.

- To become a good bunker player, some practice is required, but it needn't be arduous.

Chapter 6

On the Green

"Drive for show; putt for dough."
An old adage

We've all heard that expression about "putting for dough." And, as with many aphorisms, there's much truth in it. Reducing putts is one of the most effective ways for seniors to reduce their scores.

Putting is very individualistic. The variations seem endless because of the many options for putter lengths, putter clubheads, grips, stances, and swings.

Despite much study, I have yet to uncover the ideal way to putt—each of us must find our own "best way." To guide your choice, this chapter describes a particular putting stroke that works well for most seniors. In addition, I've provided ten specific suggestions for helping you putt more accurately. We'll start by looking at five challenges all of us need to conquer in order to improve our putting.

Challenges Facing Senior Putters

1. Plotting the right target line
2. Keeping your putter on line
3. Putting the correct distance
4. Staying tension-free
5. Coping with less than steady hands

Here are some ways to deal with these challenges.

Plotting the Right Target Line

Most good putters say that reading the green and selecting the right path to the hole is a "feel" decision. It involves more "sensing" than linear, cognitive thinking. For some players this comes naturally, but most of us need to work at (practice) relying more on our brain's uncanny ability to produce a visual image of that line.

In plotting your target line, one thing is clear; too much analysis is unproductive. It's easy to get bogged down in trying to determine the impact of a local mountain or body of water, how the grass is bent, the wind, the upward and/or downward angle of the green, how short the grass is cut, the amount of moisture or sand on the green, etcetera. Of course, we observe factors such as these, but once noticed, consider giving free reign to your brain, let it take over, and sense the right path.

I have found that my most accurate putts occur when I let my "mind's eye" do the calculating. When this happens, I can actually visualize the ball traveling from my putter to the hole. It's an incredible experience.

63

If you are not currently using this approach and would like to experiment with it, here's one possible routine:

1. Walk from your ball to the cup, observing any surface contour changes (left, right, up, down).

2. Walk around the cup, paying particular attention to the terrain within a two-foot circle of the hole.

3. While behind the hole, step back several yards, bend down, and observe the green contours with your eyes traveling from the cup back to the ball. Imagine your ball rolling from the putter to the cup.

4. Step up to putt, but give your mind ten seconds or so to process all of your observations.

5. Try to visualize the target line your mind has conjured, and confidently putt along that line.

At those times when no insight comes and you are uncertain about the target line, putt directly at the cup.

A senior strategy
Sloping Surface: Here's a helpful hint: It's called the "Krone factor." It comes into play when your path to the pin is ten feet or more and involves an obvious slope—left or right, with or without uphill or downhill components. We're not talking here about subtle changes in the green's terrain, but those that are obvious.

For many years, my friend Herman Krone, a senior golfer, observed that he consistently underestimated the amount of "bend" the ball's path took as it moved toward the hole. In effect, he ended up farther from the cup than he expected because the ball curved more sharply than anticipated.

He explains it this way:

> *"After I figure out the line I want the ball to travel, I re-aim my ball on a slightly wider path. I know it seems like a silly gimmick, but it has saved me from many a bad putt."*

If you're having trouble with these kinds of putts, Herman's idea might be worth a try.

Long putts
When plotting your line on putts of forty feet or more, it's helpful to consider three key points:

1. The relatively fast ball speed for the first portion of your putt will minimize the impact of any contours, so be careful not to overweigh them.

2. As your ball slows (last five to ten feet), contours and grass grain will have a significant influence on your ball's path. Carefully note the direction of grain and contours near the hole and factor them into your target line.

3. It can be helpful to read the line by walking from the cup back to the ball.

Quick Review

Plotting the Target Line

- Have the confidence to go with your sense or "feel" for the right line
- Observe the green contours as you walk from the cup back to the ball
- On putts of twenty-five feet or more, give careful attention to the terrain on last few feet of the target line

Keeping Your Putter on Line

Once you've determined the line you want the ball to travel, it's now critical to have the putter face strike the ball exactly perpendicular to the desired path. That's easier said than done. When seniors putt, they often, inadvertently, turn the putter head, resulting in an off-the-line putt. This happens when we make one or both of the errors listed below.

1. The clubhead is not taken in a straight back and forward motion so that the putter strikes the ball with a slight push or pull, sending the ball off the target line.

2. Hands or wrists turn as the clubhead nears or strikes the ball so that it is no longer perpendicular to the target line.

I don't know a surefire way to keep your putter on line for each putt, but I have learned a few ways that can help to keep these errors minimal. I have listed some of these ways on the following pages.

A. Use visual guides.

An effective visual guide is a **direction line** on your ball. Simply point the line at the path you want your ball to travel. Most golf balls already have a line of fine print that can serve as a direction line; some even have arrows at both ends of the printed line. An example is in Photo 6 A.

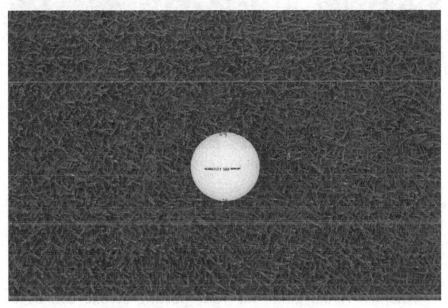

Photo 6 A

I find that if I make that golf ball line longer and bolder (maybe I need new glasses), it is easier to direct my putter head along the line's direction. To accomplish this, I use a nifty little gadget (called a "Spot Liner"), which is available in most golf shops. It is shown in Photo 6 B, along with a marked ball.

Photo 6 B

As you start your take-back, focus on the printed line so that, as you swing forward, your putter head travels in the exact direction that your ball mark is pointing.

Another visual guide for your putting stroke can be **a distinguishing spot on the green.** Ideally, you want a spot on your target line that is five to six feet ahead of your ball. This spot can be a discolored patch of grass or a repaired ball mark. I find it helpful to take a few practice strokes until my putter head swings are precisely aimed toward the selected spot.

Which is the best guideline—spot or line?
For most short putts, use the inked or printed line on the ball to align the direction of your putter stroke. For putts of twenty-five feet or more, use the "distinguishing spot" on the green to guide your putter's direction.

B. Take practice swings *behind* the ball.

Most golfers take their practice putting strokes alongside of the ball. As an alternative, seniors may find it more helpful to take their practice swings *behind* the ball—just don't ground your putter (violation of USGA rule 16, 1e). In other words, address the ball, but for practice, swing your putter head behind it (in the direction of your target line). Photo 6 C shows such a practice position. This is a great way to be certain that your putter is being swung perpendicular to the target line. As you take your practice swings, carefully watch the path traveled by your putter. It's relatively easy to spot a stroke that has a slight arc or curve instead of remaining perfectly square to your target line. Loosely tucking your elbows close to your sides is helpful in keeping your putter on a straight path.

Keep at the practice strokes until you correct whatever is causing the deviation. Then, confidently step up to the ball, and make your putt.

Photo 6 C

C. Keep head and eyes directly over the ball.

We all know this, so what's the big deal? Well, "the big deal" is that it's easy to be fooled. We believe our head/eyes are over the ball even when they are not. An analysis of my own setup is that I tend to place my head and eyes, not over the ball, but someplace between my feet and the ball. When this happens, I am likely to push the ball left of my target line (for righties, it will go to the right).

How well do you keep your eyes directly over the ball? Want to try a simple test? Here's one you can do at home:

1. Tie a key or any small weight on the end of a three-foot string.
2. Set up as if to putt—golf ball in place and putter in hand. Address the ball so that your eyes are directly over it (or at least it seems that way to you).
3. Keeping one hand on the putter, use your other hand to place the unweighted end of the string on the bridge of your nose, right between your eyes. Now look to see where the weight lines up (see Photo 6 D).
4. If the weight does not align itself right over the ball, move your feet so that it does.

You now have a sense for what it looks/feels like to have your head directly over the ball.

Select a visual cue to help guide you to this position when actually putting. For example, I find that my eyes are directly over the ball when the toes of my shoes are about ten inches from the ball (see Photo 6 E). I use this ten-inch guide every time I putt.

Photo 6 D   Photo 6 E

D. Eliminate all movement except for your shoulders.
Fewer moving parts means less chance for error. So it's helpful to eliminate weight shifts, wrist action, or head movement. One way to achieve this is to move your putter by an up and down movement of your shoulders—left shoulder down, then right shoulder down (right-handers). This allows your arms to swing like a pendulum.

Strive to have your hands and arms feeling loose and relaxed. Your hands and arms (coming down from your shoulders) should form a "V." This "V" is kept intact from setup, to backstroke, to forward swing.

A subtle but important part of this putting stroke is the *slight* upward cock of your wrists. That is, instead of grasping the putter with your hands hanging straight down, you elevate your fingertips about an inch. This slight, upward wrist cock provides increased "feel" or sensitivity in judging how firmly to strike the ball; it also helps keep your putter on a straight track.

The distance the putt must travel determines the length of the backswing. I find that my putt speed is most accurate when the length of the follow-through roughly equals the length of the backstroke.

Give it a try.
The putting stroke we've just described is not limited to use by seniors; most pros use some variation of it. However, over the years, having experimented with many putting strokes, I find that as an aging golfer I am more consistently on line with the shoulder-movement method than any others I've tried. For this reason, I recommend that seniors test it against their present putting technique.

When you first try this putting stroke, it may seem a bit awkward. However, with a little practice on the putting green, you may be surprised how smoothly it goes. You will like your accuracy.

E. A still head.
Before leaving this section on putting and body movement, please grant me the liberty of reminding you about the absolute need to keep your head still—well past the time you strike the ball. I usually don't have the discipline to keep my head still until

I hear the ball drop into the cup, but I try. Not turning your head is particularly important with long putts because of the great temptation to look up as the ball is being struck. Unfortunately, this slight movement often takes the putter head off the desired line.

Quick Review

Keeping Your Putter on Line

- **Use visual guides**
- **Take practice swings, on the target line, *behind the* ball**
- **Head and eyes directly over the ball**
- **Eliminate all movement except shoulders**
- **Work at keeping head still**

Putting the Correct Distance

"Never up; never in" is one of golf's truisms. We all understand the problem of leaving the ball short of the hole. But hitting the ball too hard leads to rimming out, bouncing over the hole, or running well past the cup. Many golf experts say that accurate distance is more important than the line, especially on long putts. On the putting green, most seniors will benefit greatly by allocating half of the practice time to putts of twenty-five feet or more.

Some suggestions for hitting your putt the correct distance are:

A. Imagine rolling the ball with an underhand toss.

As you stand behind your ball and look at the hole, try to imagine how hard you would swing your arm (underhanded) in order to roll your ball to the cup. Eliminate any wrist action in this imaginary toss. This kinesthetic feel will help you judge the speed of your putting stroke, particularly if you follow the suggestion in the next paragraph.

B. Use your back hand as your primary guide.

Clearly, there are many ways to stroke your putt. However, this one works best for me: I use my left hand (since I am left-handed) to guide the take-back, hit, and follow-through. My right hand more or less comes along for the ride. Using your dominant hand/arm to guide the stroke takes advantage of your lifetime experiences in using that arm for tossing balls and other objects.

C. Pay close attention to downward slopes.

More often than not, I underestimate the distance the ball will travel on downward slopes (i.e., I hit it too hard). This error usually occurs when I fail to pay attention to the direction of the grain. As you know, balls traveling in the same direction as the grain travel faster (farther) than balls running against or cross the grain. This knowledge is important because *grass blades almost always bend downhill* and *not,* as is commonly believed, toward the westerly sun. Surprised?

Another mistake I make is not recognizing subtle downhill changes in the slope. I've learned to avoid this error by walking from my ball to the hole and a bit beyond, all the while looking carefully for mounds or slight declines.

D. Don't dawdle.

My experience has been that standing a long time over a putt rarely improves accuracy. While we're standing there, we're likely to start thinking about the factors that might affect the putt (slope, green's surface, the distance, etcetera). Too much analyzing often leads to a diminishment of confidence. At worst, we get uptight and have the yips.

The time to do your thinking and planning is before you step up to the ball. That's when you determine your target line. This often can be accomplished while others are putting. Once you've determined your target line, try not to second-guess yourself. Step up, take a few practice swings, and confidently go for it.

Quick Review

Putting the Correct Distance

- **Imagine rolling the ball underhanded to the pin**
- **Use your back hand as primary guide**
- **Pay careful attention to downward slopes**
- **Practice putts of twenty-five yards or longer each time you play a round**
- **Don't dawdle over a putt**

Staying Tension Free

It's your turn to putt on the eighteenth hole. Sink it, and you and your partner win the match; miss it and ... talk about pressure! But, as every golfer knows, it doesn't need to be an eighteenth-hole situation to induce anxiety—putting is one of the most stressful shots in golf.

The problem is that accurate putting requires that you be confident and relaxed. While being at ease is important for all golf shots, it's more essential when putting. So, how do you deal with the stress when you are faced with that important putt? Here are a few suggestions:

A.Make sure your hands are loose.
As you step up to address the ball, focus on your hands. If you feel any tightness, don't proceed with the putt. Sometimes wriggling your fingers will reduce the tension. Bob Marier, a low-handicap golfer friend of mine, put it this way:

"Imagine cradling a baby chick in your hands. That same looseness and gentleness should be experienced as you are about to putt."

B. Get confident about the line.

Look at your putt from both sides of the cup. Do you get a sense for how the ball will move? If you're not certain, ask for your partner's or caddy's input. Thinking about the line needn't be a long process, but you do need to "noodle it" enough to reach a comfortable conclusion. As was mentioned earlier, go with whatever your "mind's eye" is telling you. If you are uncertain about the direction or speed of your putt, you'll find it difficult to be relaxed.

Senior strategy

Adopt a "what the hell" attitude. If after trying the ideas mentioned above you still feel uncomfortable about your putt, console yourself with the thought that probably no one else can figure it out either. Just shrug your shoulders and go ahead and stroke your putt.

Walk away from it. Let's say you have to make a short putt, but it's an important one (perhaps a chance for a birdie). In that kind of situation, it's easy to get the yips—you don't feel at ease and your practice stroke is a bit jerky. That's the time to walk away from the putt, dangle your arms and shake your hands a few times to relax your muscles, take a few deep breaths, and then go back and putt away.

Walking away from a putt is often difficult for me because I tend to be impatient and want to get on with things. But, I've finally learned to discipline myself to not proceed with the putt when I feel tense. Postponing your putt, even for thirty seconds, may be just the action that helps you sink it.

Quick Review

Staying Tension Free

- **Get confident about the line**
- **Adopt a "what the hell" attitude**
- **When uncomfortable, walk away from putt**
- **Be sure hands are loose**

Unsteady Hands

As we age, many of us develop slight hand tremors or discover that we are less skillful with delicate hand/arm movements. Using a long putter is one way to cope with these physical changes.

George, one of my golfer friends said this:

"I had a bad case of the yips. The longer putter helped me smooth out my stroke."

Most of the long/belly putter users that I interviewed say that this kind of putter made a significant improvement in their ability to send the ball down their selected target line. If your putting has deteriorated a bit, the belly or a long putter might be worth a try. Even if you have steady hands, you might want to experiment. Currently on the PGA Tour there is an increasing use of the belly and long putters—not only by seniors but by young, fast-rising professionals. I'm going to give one a whirl myself.

On the Green—Summary

- Let your "mind's eye" determine the target line.

- When hands are less than steady, consider using a belly or long putter.

- The key to successful putting is being confident and relaxed.

- There is no one, ideal way to putt. Each of us needs to find a stroke that works well most of the time.

- Accurate putting means keeping your putter head perpendicular to the target line. Some ways to achieve this are:

    1. Use visual guidelines

    2. Take practice swings along the target line.

    3. Keep you eyes directly over the ball.

    4. During putting stroke, eliminate all movement except for your shoulders.

- Don't dawdle over your putts. If you feel uncertain, take a few deep breaths and set up again.

- When determining your target path for long putts, place more weight on how the green slopes on the last half of the distance (as the ball slows) rather than on the first half.

Chapter 7

It's All in Your Head

> Golf is the only sport in which the most feared opponent is you.

Players quickly learn that golf is a "head" game.

You don't have to be Sigmund to know that what's going on in your mind affects your body and vice versa.

Jennifer's experience is a good example:

Jennifer sliced her drive into the rough. While this was a bit upsetting, the real pressure came when she and her partners couldn't immediately find her ball. As they were looking, Jennifer could see the next foursome waiting, seemingly impatiently, on the tee box. Finally, the ball was found (with a pretty good lie), and when it became her turn to hit, she rushed the shot, topped it, and the ball remained in the rough. Ouch!

Sound familiar? Tension makes a good swing almost impossible. Ken Raynor, golf pro at Cape Arundel Golf Club, in

Kennebunkport, Maine, showed me a graphic example of how tension can mess up hitting the ball. He had me address a ball with my 7-iron, grounding the club behind the ball as in preparation for a swing. Then, he said, "Jack, tighten up your forearms a little—as if you were anxious." Immediately, involuntarily, the club lifted off the ground, so if I had then swung the club, the heavy part of the clubhead would have struck the middle or upper half of the ball, resulting in a topped shot. Most likely, this is what caused Jennifer's miss-hit. Tension can be sneaky.

Tension can lead to all sorts of swing mishaps. Here are a few that most seniors experience:

- Rushed shot—loss of rhythm
- Tight hands or wrists—loss of distance
- Too short a backswing
- Jerking a putting stroke
- Overly cautious swing
- Arms moved ahead of body turn

In this chapter we'll discuss the sources of most golf course tension and provide suggestions for reducing anxious, uptight feelings. The key antidote for tension is keeping our mind in a positive mode—remaining self-confident. Let's start by looking at the sources of golf tensions.

For most golfers, tension comes from two sources:

A. Internal, self-generated pressures.
Your thoughts trigger the anxiety. For example: You're having a bad round and start "talking to yourself" about what you need

to do to correct things. As you try to correct your swing, tension builds, and your shots remain "off."

B. External Pressures.
Something or somebody on the course gets the juices flowing. For example: the club pro and several of his/her friends are standing by the first tee box when you're about to tee off. You want to "look good" so you become cautious and, as a result, fail to take a full backswing. Your drive ends up being short and in the rough.

Self-Generated Pressures

Sometimes we're our own worst enemies. Even though I am a psychologist, I am subject to the same self-induced pressures as every other golfer. Fortunately, I've found some ways to minimize them. Here they are:

A. Keep self-confident.
The amount of tension or anxiety we experience depends upon how confident we feel. When we're sure of ourselves, we're usually physically relaxed, and our swing seems "grooved." As one of my golfer friends puts it, "You're in the zone."

So why aren't we this confident more of the time? Why do we lose our confidence? After all, it's just a game. Or is it? This is the heart of the matter. For most of us, playing golf is more than "just a game." It's us against the course; our ego and sense of self-worth are being challenged. If you are competitive by nature, the you-versus-the-course pressure is intensified. But, regardless of competitive level, most golfers want to do well, and when we are not succeeding, our confidence can quickly erode. Here's a typical example:

> *You begin the round with several good holes—the chips are landing close to the pin, and the putts are dropping. Perhaps you're playing couples golf and simply are out to enjoy a social game, or maybe you're with a few close friends that aren't too serious about the game. Whatever the case, you start out comfortably confident because there's little pressure from your companions. You're relaxed. Then, you get to the par 5 seventh hole, and, surprisingly, slice your drive out of bounds. You struggle through the rest of the hole and end up with an eight. How does the rest of the match go? If you're like most seniors, it doesn't go as well as before. Your confidence has now been shaken; you become a little uptight, perhaps swing too fast, and are off-target on shots to the green that are usually a cinch.*

Sound familiar? Fortunately, we can do something about it. In the items below are suggestions for maintaining a good confidence level.

B. Get realistic.

Of course it's disappointing to slice out of bounds, but why does it impact so much on our ego and devastate our confidence? A big part of the answer rests in our expectations. Most of us expect that each shot should be good—after all, we know we can make it—we've hit it well plenty of times before. When this unconscious expectation of doing well on every shot is not met, it leads to frustration, reduced confidence, and tension.

When you think about it, it seems incredible that we have expectations of perfection. The best pros don't play consistently well, despite constant practice and an accompanying coach. One weekend Phil Mickelson won a PGA tournament, and two weeks later he failed to make the cut. Golf is such a difficult game that it is impossible to be consistent.

To minimize anxiety from poorly played holes, establish more realistic expectations for your day-to-day play. Let's face it, on any given round, most seniors are apt to have miss-hits, sliced shots, messed-up bunker attempts, or other mishaps. The expectation that every shot will be hit satisfactorily is crazy—even the pros can't perform at that level.

C. Change your expectations.

The good news is that you can change your expectations and, in turn, significantly preserve your confidence (and play better).

When your expectations are realistic, the instances when they are unfulfilled will be few, and the occasions of tension less. A good way to begin changing your expectations is to estimate the average number of bad holes you have per round. For example, if your average score is 96, it's likely that you have four to five holes in which you score a double bogie (or worse). So, be realistic and set your expectation that you'll not be perfect—that you'll mess up four to five holes.

With your new expectation of five "bad" holes, your reaction now will be different when you screw one up. Instead of getting frustrated or angry, simply say to yourself, "Well, that's one of my bad holes—let's move on to the next." In effect, you accept the fact that such holes will happen and continue on with your play. Who knows, by not becoming upset when you experience a bad hole, you may experience fewer of them (than anticipated) for the rest of the round.

D. Relish your successes.
When you perform well on a hole, enjoy the moment.

On courses you play frequently, there may be one hole that usually gives you a "hard time." For me, it's a 175-yard par 3 that requires a long carry over swamp and water. When I get over the hazard and land near the green, I try to bask in the pleasure of the accomplishment. I give myself an "atta-boy" and silently tell myself, "You're doing okay."

Positive self-talks such as these can help you remain upbeat despite other mishaps.

E. Use "comfortable" clubs.
Another way to keep your tension minimal is to stick with clubs that you feel confident in using. If your fairway metal rarely works well for you, but you can almost always count on a good shot with your hybrid club, use the hybrid. You may not hit the ball quite as far, but more consistently, you'll be down the fairway in a spot that nicely sets up your next shot. Moreover, this next shot is likely to be good because you're not experiencing the tension that follows a poor hit. The best place to get better at using "difficult" clubs is on the practice range, not during your round of golf.

F. Have some fun—make enjoyment your objective.
Many seniors play golf for "exercise" or "to get out in the air," but almost all of us also play with the hope of having some fun. And, the best part is that when you're enjoying yourself, you're likely

to be relaxed and play better. Here are some ideas for keeping your focus on enjoyment:

Forget about the score. Did you ever play a round without keeping score? If you haven't, try it. It can be a very freeing experience. If you're not counting your strokes, it's easier to be cavalier about errant shots. I guarantee you'll enjoy the round. If you can't bring yourself to not record your strokes, let someone else keep the scorecard and don't ask about scores until the round is over.

Play with people who are fun to be with. Sometimes this is not possible if you play in a league or with a business group. However, to the degree you can control with whom you play, it's to your advantage. For example, when I'm in a foursome with a very slow player, it is easy for me to get impatient and become uptight. Do some of the people you play with contribute to your being tense or uncomfortable?

To the extent possible, set up rounds with others who are fun to be with. For me, it's usually guys that laugh easily and don't take their game too seriously. My wife and I also have fun playing together because we support and encourage each other. We also enjoy playing with other couples that play at our level.

Finding the right people to play with is an important factor in scoring better.

Put the Bad Shots/Holes Aside. This is not easy to do. For most of us, there is a perverse element in our makeup that leads us to dwell on our failures. At times, my wife can't get to sleep at night because her mind keeps replaying a poor hole or round. Dwelling on our mistakes is a sure way to destroy confidence. Here's what we can do about it:

- **Treat it as a learning experience.** View the bad hole/round as an opportunity for improvement. Given the chance to play the same round over, what would you do differently? Take that analysis to the practice range or to a golf pro for a constructive lesson. These are positive steps that can help you gain confidence in your ability to conquer the problem.

- **Dwell on the positive.** Recall the good shots you had. It can be helpful to focus on two or three that went especially well and review in your mind how each was accomplished—what was good about your swing, how you finished, what it felt like as the ball headed toward your target, etcetera. Positive imaging can definitely help combat tension and even increase your self-confidence.

    For greater impact, review each day's round, focusing on those shots that went well. For example, as you go to bed, review in your mind each hole, centering in on the really good shots. The bet is that you will be amazed at how many you had—the net effect being a heightened level of self-confidence.

- **Don't carry yesterday's baggage.** Tomorrow brings a new day and the likelihood things will be better. How many times have you had a disappointing round, only to find that the next time you played those difficulties vanished? One way to help rid yourself of yesterday's bad shots is to talk them out—get them off your chest. Complain to someone who is a sympathetic listener. It's amazing how freeing that can be.

- **Look at the big picture.** When all else fails, it's helpful to keep in perspective the fact that there are real problems in this life; a poor round of golf is not one of them. Remind yourself of the good fortune to be playing on this side of the grass and the gift it is to be physically able to play the game. And, focus on the fact that there's always another day!

Quick Review

Reducing Self-Generated Tension

- **Self-confidence is the key to lower scores**
- **Set more realistic expectations for your round**
- **Relish your successes**
- **Use comfortable clubs**
- **Make enjoyment your objective**
- **Forget about scores**
- **Play with persons you enjoy being with**
- **Put a bad shot/hole behind you. Focus ahead**
- **Dwell on positive images of successful shots**
- **Put the game in perspective—there is more to life than golf**

Externally Generated Pressures

In this part, we'll consider some strategies for coping with three potentially tension-creating situations often encountered while playing.

A. Facing a significant hazard.

Let's say you're playing a course for the first time. Suddenly, you come upon a scary hazard. It could be a wide expanse of water, a swamp, or some imposing weed-filled area from which it would be impossible to hit a shot (if you don't carry the hazard). Photo 7 A is a typical hazard of this sort.

Photo 7 A

We'll assume that you are capable of hitting the ball over the hazard span, but as you look at it, your confidence begins to wane; you become a little anxious and perhaps can even detect some slight muscle tension. You're wishing you could substitute a "water ball" for the one you're playing with. Sound familiar?

Here are some ways to minimize the tension:

1. **Take more club than you think you'll need.** When we're concerned about clearing a hazard, there is often a temptation to swing harder "to make sure I get over it." That harder swing usually leads to a miss-hit. Instead of the faster swing, take a club or two more than you think you'll need and swing slowly and smoothly, confident in the knowledge that you've got "plenty of club."

2. **Erase the negative self-talk.** When faced with a difficult shot, one that brings with it even a tiny bit of concern, we often, unconsciously, begin talking to ourselves. These little self-talks are usually negative: "I hate water hazards," "I hope I don't top the ball," "A miss here will devastate my good score," etcetera. The reality is that if you think you might not succeed with the shot, the likelihood is that you'll botch it.

   You erase the negative thoughts by substituting positive-self talk. One way to accomplish this is to think about successes you've had in similar situations. For example:

   "I almost always get over the water on our thirteenth hole, and this is no worse; in fact, it's easier. What am I worried about? I can do it."

> *"I'm glad I chose a longer club; this way I'll swing easily and won't stress myself."*

> *"The worst that can happen is I'll have to take a penalty, but, even so, I still can salvage a bogie out of it."*

3. **Focus on Positive Images.** Another way to help erase negative thoughts is to focus on positive images. Visualize your ball sailing over the hazard and onto the far fairway or green. Try to take your focus off the swing and redirect it toward a successful result. This takes discipline, but when you visualize how your good shot will look, your mind unconsciously guides your body to produce it.

    To help develop this positive visualization, think of a time when you hit a great shot of similar length. What did it look and feel like? One of my frequently called upon visual memories is of a 6-iron shot I hit from 150 yards to about three feet from the pin. I can see myself taking a slow, full backswing and then slowly turning my body to propel the club. Recalling that shot always brings a smile to my face, especially as I remember the comment of one of my playing partners, who said, "That's a shot of a five-handicapper." At that time, my course handicap was twenty.

Quick Review

Reducing Tension When Facing a Hazard

- **Take more club than usual**
- **Generate positive self-talks**
- **Visualize your shot clearing the hazard**

B. Pressure from the group behind.

Sometimes you're in a situation in which the foursome behind you seems to be constantly waiting. If this occurs at only a couple of holes, it usually doesn't become a problem, but if it is more frequent, subtle pressure can easily begin to build. In turn, this is likely to lead to hurried swings and/or rushed putts. Not good. Here are a few ways to cope with this kind of pressure:

1. **Check it out.** While the foursome behind may be waiting on most holes, they may not be feeling at all impatient or irritated with the speed of your group's play. The only way to determine this is to ask, "Would you like to play through?" If they say, "No, we're in no hurry," then the pressure is off. Relax and enjoy your round. If they say, "Yes, thank you," let them through. Most of the time it's far better to play a little longer round than to be experiencing pressure that throws off your game.

2. **Ask your playing partners to "pick up the pace."** I like to play fast, so I typically imagine those waiting behind us are getting impatient with the

speed of our play. However, my playing partners may not even be aware of the pressure I am experiencing. I often have to point out the waiting foursome and ask our group to speed up—"Can we pick up the pace?" or "Let's play ready-golf—they've been waiting for us on almost every hole."

3. **Use self-talks.** If your efforts at speeding up the play are falling on deaf ears, you now need to deal with your own self-generated stress. Once again, self-talks can help, for example:

   "I can't do anything about it, so I'm just going to play my game." Or, *"It's just me making myself uptight; I don't have to let this situation control me. I'll make this next swing slow and relaxed.*

4. **Unload on one of your partners.** You can rid yourself of anxious feelings by talking them out. For instance, as you are walking up the fairway, you might say to one of your partners, "I feel uncomfortable with that group waiting for us all the time—it makes me tense. Does it bother you any?" She might respond, "Yeah, it does a little bit; maybe we can get the others to speed up." Even if your group doesn't substantially "speed up," the act of talking out your feelings often frees you from them. In effect, they are out of your head and less likely to impact on your play.

Quick Review

Reducing Tension When Pressured from Group Behind

- **Check it out**
- **Ask partners to pick up pace**
- **Self-talk away the pressure**
- **Unload your anxious feelings**

C. Sudden rain.

I usually won't start a round if it's raining. But sometimes when I'm partway through a round, the drops begin, and my partners want to continue to play. In such a situation it's easy for seniors, myself included, to become uncomfortable or distressed.

Before we discuss managing rain-induced pressure, don't overlook the fact that we can minimize our physical discomfort by carrying items to help stay dry. Here are four items in my bag:

- Rain jacket
- Extra glove—especially one designed for wet weather
- Umbrella
- Towel

Rain play and mental set

How well you play in the rain depends a lot on your attitude about the situation. If your usual reaction to rain is one of irritation or disgust, it results in a mental set that can become self-defeating. Thoughts such as, "I can't play in this stuff," Or, "I hate it when my glove is wet," will not lead to good results.

Instead, make a conscious effort to accept the rain simply as another hazard. Sure, it's no fun playing in rain, but it's also no fun hitting into a water hazard or having to tee off directly into a strong wind. We seem to accept these conditions as "part of the game" and roll with them. We can react in like manner when rain begins. To keep a positive attitude, I find it helpful to classify the rain as simply another golf challenge that needs to be conquered. I engage in little self-talks about "not letting it beat me," and "maybe my competitors are more upset than I am, and I'll win the round."

In a nutshell, do whatever you can to avoid making the rain an enemy. If you can't beat it, join it. It doesn't pay to focus on things over which you have no control; rain is one of them. Who knows, perhaps after the next hole your partners will say "enough is enough," and you all can go to the nineteenth hole for a warming drink.

Quick Review

Coping With Sudden Rain

- **Stock bag with rain gear**
- **Accept rain as just another hazard**
- **Talk self into not letting it "get to you"**

It's All in Your Head—Summary

- Muscles that are relaxed and free of tension are essential for a good swing.

- Much tension on the course is self-generated, usually stemming from loss of confidence.

- We lose confidence when we perceive ourselves as doing poorly. However, none of us can be perfect at golf. If our benchmark is an unrealistic expectation that every shot should be good—that we "should have done better"—it is almost impossible to remain confident.

- To reduce incidents of lowered confidence, develop more realistic expectations, so that when a bad hole or shot occurs, we don't do "a number on ourselves."

- Hitting shots with clubs that you feel comfortable with can help retain confidence and keep tension from creeping into the round.

- Positive self-talks and positive visual images about times you have hit well can help counteract loss of confidence.

- Make the goal for your golf day to be one of enjoyment. Playing with others who are fun to be with can help you stay relaxed and be more confident about your game.

- When you have a round in which putts or chips or drives let you down, minimize your negative thoughts by recognizing that you can overcome the problem. Go to a golf pro or practice range to find ways to improve.

- Don't take golf too seriously—it's just a game. Think about the wonderful gift it is to be able to play eighteen holes.

Chapter 8

Practicing Golf
Senior Style

To get better, you don't have to practice a lot, but you do have to practice.

I asked three of my senior golfing friends. "What do you do, if anything, about practicing golf?" Here's what they said:

"I don't bother practicing much. If I practice just before I play, it gets me loosened up, but it also tires me. I only go to the range at other times if I'm having a big problem."

"I go to the practice range once in awhile, but it gets tedious. One basket of balls is plenty for me."

"I don't see a lot of carryover from the range to the course. It's not worth spending a lot of time on practicing."

I don't know whether or not those sentiments reflect your experience, but I would bet that a majority of seniors don't invest much time or effort on the practice range. When I interview senior golfers and ask why they don't practice more, their answers come down to two basic reasons:

1. Lack of easy access/proximity to a driving range.

2. Limited growth or progress, despite the practice. That is, there seems to be little payback (lower scores) for the energy invested.

Getting a Better Payback from Practice

In this book, we can't help much with item #1 above, but here are some suggestions for making senior golf practice more productive:

1. **Do practice regularly.** Not every day, but once a week is a reasonable goal. On the course, it is almost impossible to make changes that lead to improved scores; there is always the pressure not to screw up, and so experimentation is curtailed. If you are having trouble—slicing, hooking, topping, weak fairway shots, whatever—the driving range is the place to work at finding solutions. Sometimes just fifteen minutes of effort provides the answer. I know many seniors who never practice, but the best golfers I know consistently practice. 'nuff said?

2. **Spend time on shots that make the greatest difference.** Sure it's fun to take our driver to see how far and accurately we can hit it, but unless

your drives are uncommonly bad, a greater return for time invested can come from improved short iron shots, chipping, and putting. Becoming more accurate with shots to the green reduces your putts, and that, in turn, makes a big impact on your score. So, at the range or in your yard, spend most of your effort on the short game.

3. **Always have a specific target.** If you are going to practice chipping, for example, set a pail or basket thirty or so yards away and try to get as many balls as possible in/near the basket.

4. **Define exactly what you want to improve.** It does little good simply to hit balls, even if you have a target. You need to be clear about what you hope to change in your swing. For instance, if you notice, when chipping to the basket that you frequently top the ball, then your goal for the practice session would be to find some mechanism that keeps your head steady and consistently allows you to strike down on the ball. Experiment with different swings until your ball flies high in the air (hint: make sure your weight is on your front foot). If you can't solve the problem, ask a PGA pro for guidance. In any case, before hitting the range, ask yourself, "What do I specifically want to change or improve upon?" Stick with that goal for the entire practice session.

5. **Don't limit your practice to the range.** Backyards can be used for chipping practice, a high-ceiling room or garage can provide space to "groove"

a swing (without hitting a ball), and a smooth carpet can help with your putting stroke. In these convenient locations, you can work at mentally becoming comfortable with any swing adjustments you may have made. Practicing swings, even without a ball, can help develop the right muscle memory to carry with you to the course.

6. **Consult a pro early on.** If initial attempts to improve fail, don't spin your wheels. Consult a pro that can put you on the right path. Unless you can view a film of your swing, it is difficult to analyze by yourself what is wrong or needs to be changed. If, after your lesson and some practice, you find yourself frustrated at not successfully implementing the change, don't delay in going back to the pro. Most significant swing changes usually require one or two additional lessons to help us from slipping back to our old ways.

7. **Make the practice fun.** Practice sessions needn't be tedious. One way to make them enjoyable is to limit your time on the range. One pail of balls or twenty minutes is enough for most seniors. A second help is to use reasonable, measurable goals so that you can experience a sense of satisfaction when you achieve the desired result. For example, "out of the next ten balls, my goal is to hit five that don't slice." If you happen to be practicing with a friend, make little bets on "who can get closest to the one-hundred-yard marker" or whatever target you are working with.

Practicing Golf Senior Style—Summary

- Practice is necessary if you want to improve your scores.

- Most of the practice time should be spent on the short game.

- Make practice an enjoyable experience. You can accomplish this by limiting your practice time to twenty minutes, by setting specific objectives for the session, and by making a "game" of the practice.

Chapter 9

Games Seniors Play

Golf should be fun. What can make it more fun for you?

Golf is a great game in and of itself. We enjoy playing it for the challenges it provides as well as those glory moments when we chip in, birdie, or smash an incredible drive. So, do we need any additional games?

The answer is, "We don't." But, golf games—side bets—can add to your pleasure. Games provide an extra dimension to a round—especially if you usually play with the same group of friends. The fun stems from the competition—not only from beating the course, but also in beating your partners. Games also add to enjoyment by providing another avenue for winning—something that brings a quiet pleasure.

The key to keeping the games fun is to play for low stakes. For example, a loss might mean buying the beer or paying out a few bucks. When stakes are high or meaningful, pressure enters the scene and enjoyment diminishes. The idea is not to make money, but to add a little zest to the round.

Games for Seniors to Play

Six, Six, Six

Players Needed: Four

How it Works:
During the round, each player partners for six holes with each of the other players. To start off, use any format to select for first pairings. Our group, for instance, hits off the first tee and then the longest ball hitter pairs up with the shortest ball hitter. This is repeated as we tee off for the seventh hole. Of course, no repetitions are allowed—every player must play six holes with each of the other three golfers.

Scoring:
Match play. The best ball for each team determines which group wins the hole. Individual scores can be based on handicaps or not.

Each six-hole set—one through six, seven through twelve, and thirteen through eighteen—is considered a "round." The team that wins the most holes during a round is declared winner for that round. Depending upon the agreed-upon stakes per round, the losers pay the winners, and a new round is begun with new two-person combination.

A variation on the six-hole round is to divide each of the six holes into "front" and "back" nines (i.e., the first three holes represent the front nine; the second three the back nine).

Example: Your team won two of the first three holes, so you won the "front" nine and the other team owes each of you a dollar. On the next three holes, each team won a hole and one hole was halved, so no blood. No money is owed. If your team wins both the front and back nine, the other team owes each of the winners two dollars for that six-hole round.

Nines

Players Needed: Three

How It Works:
For each hole, each player earns points

Hole winner	= 5 Points
Second	= 3 Points
Last	= 1 Point

If all players get the same score, points are divided 3, 3, and 3. If one wins and the other two tie, points are divided 5, 2, and 2. Total points given must always add up to nine. The person with the most points at the end of eighteen holes is the winner.

Payouts can be a "kitty" agreed upon before the match begins. For example, everyone puts up two dollars, and the winner walks away with six dollars.

Another way is to agree on how much a point is worth—ten cents a point is a common amount. At the end of the round, let's say that Susan has 64 points, John has 57, and Bob has 41. In this case, John pays Susan $ .70 (64 – 57 = 7 x $ .10 = $.70) and Bob needs to pay her $2.30 (64 – 41 = 23).

Nassau

Players Needed: Two or four

How It Works:
Think of a nassau as three tournaments in one—the front nine, the back nine, and the entire eighteen holes each represent a separate bet. It can be played as individuals or as two-person teams. It can be match or stroke play.

Whichever team (or person) wins the front nine gets a prize; whatever team (or person) wins the back nine gets a prize, and the team/player with the lowest eighteen-hole total gets a prize.

A commonly used nassau is the two dollar nassau. Each of the two nines is worth two dollars, and the eighteen-hole total is worth two dollars. If some team or player sweeps all the categories, they win six dollars.

Pressing:
A team or player, who is losing a nine by two or more holes, can "press." In effect, the losing team/player (at some point before the end of the nine) asks the winning team or players to open a new bet. If those ahead accept the challenge, and should win, the pressing team owes not two dollars for the nine, but must pay up four dollars. If the pressing team wins the nine, then they win four dollars for that nine. The amount of the press is usually the same as the original nassau.

Skins

Players Needed: Works best with three or four

How it Works:
Skins is a game of match play in which players agree beforehand how much each hole is worth. A typical friendly skins game might value each hole as being worth a dollar. If you win a hole, you win a skin. There is no winner, for a hole, if two or more tie for the best score.

Skins play can become exciting because if no one wins a hole, the dollar is carried over to the next hole; if no one wins that hole, it carries over to the third, and so on. If, for example, no one wins after four holes, the next hole would be worth five dollars (four dollars for the past four holes and one dollar for the hole being played).

In this example, each of the other players, let's say three, owe the winner five dollars. Money usually does not pass hands until the match if over, and then the amount owed each player is calculated.

Side Bets—Sometimes Referred to as "Garbage" or "Junk"

Some players don't like side bets because they can become a distraction; others see "garbage" as a fun way to get rewarded for good play. You and your group will have to decide whether they add to the enjoyment of your rounds. If you decide to add side bets to your round, you can use as many different bets as is agreed upon.

With our regular group, the winner of each side bet wins fifty cents. We'll use that amount in our examples, but your group can choose any amount that you mutually agree upon. Again, keep in mind that a low amount is usually best for everyone's enjoyment.

Here are six garbage possibilities:

The garbage games to be played, as well as the dollar amount to be awarded the winners, is agreed upon before the match begins.

Greeny or Pins: Greenies take place on par 3 holes. A greeny is won when a player's drive lands on the green and then he/she makes par. If two or more players drive the green and make par, the greeny is awarded to the one whose drive ended up closest to the pin.

If no one has a greeny on the first par 3 hole, it may be agreed to "carry over" the greeny to subsequent par 3 holes until someone gets a greeny. In such a case, instead of winning fifty cents, the player wins fifty cents for each of the prior holes for which no one made a greeny. For example, if on the first two par 3s, no one scored a greeny, then the greeny winner on the third par 3 wins $1.50.

Sandy: A sandy occurs when a player hits out of a bunker and, on the next shot, makes par.

Chippy: A chippy occurs when a player hits from off the green, and the ball falls into the cup.

Ellliot: A par 5 bet devised by Elliot Speers, a golfer at Webhannet Golf Club in Kennebunk, Maine. To win an Elliot, a player must reach a par 5 hole in three (or less) strokes and also make par. If two or more get on in three, the one whose ball was closest to the pin (and makes par) wins the Elliot. Only one player can win.

Gus: Good for long par 3s when each player's drive fails to get on the green. You win a "Gus" when, on the second shot, you come closest to the pin and also par the hole. It was conceived by Gus Wilson, one of my golfing buddies.

Arnie: Value for this side bet should be determined before the round starts. An Arnie is won by any golfer who makes par without having landed his/her ball on the fairway. Named in honor of Arnold Palmer, who made quite a few Arnies during his career.

Games Seniors Play—Summary

"Games" can add enjoyment to a round of golf. They are simply small bets that work well when stakes are kept low. The idea is not to make money, but to add zest to the round.

- Two-player game (or four players divided into two teams)
  - o Nassau

- Four-player games:
  - o Six, Six, Six
  - o Nassau
  - o Skins

- Three-player game:
  - o Nines
  - o Skins

- Side bets or "garbage"
  - o Greeny
  - o Sandy
  - o Chippy
  - o Elliot
  - o Gus
  - o Arnie

About the Author

John Drake is a psychologist and author. He has seven published books to his credit, including the best-selling, award-winning *Downshifting* (Berrett-Koehler), currently published in ten languages.

John also knows senior golfers and their needs. He is an avid golfer who plays left-handed and carries a GHIN Handicap Index of 16.9. This year, at age eighty, he won his club's member-guest and member-member tournaments. Having played the game for more than twenty-five years, his considerable trial-and-error experience is incorporated into *How to Drop Five Strokes....* In addition, his psychological insights can help seniors cope with the mental side of the game.

Dr. Drake's wife is also a golfer. Observing and discussing her play enabled the author to address many problems confronted by senior female golfers.

Earlier in life, John was the founder and CEO of one of the world's largest human resources firms, Drake Beam and Associates Inc., now DBM Inc., with offices in forty-three countries. As a relatively young man, he sold this firm and established two more companies. Finally, when he "retired," he turned his talents to writing. He has a PhD in psychology and is a well-known consultant and lecturer in the corporate arena.

John and Dee Drake have four sons. They divide their time between Maine and Florida.

Glossary

Terms Used in This Book

belly putter: A putter having a long shaft. Some golfers place the top of the shaft against their belly or chest; others use similar putters but keep the top of shaft in their hand slightly away from their body.

bump-and-run: A shot, usually to the green, in which the ball is kept low, bounces a few times, and rolls toward the target.

chip: A short shot to the green.

chippy: Basically, it's a chip-in. A shot in which the player hits anywhere from off the green, and the ball drops into the cup. Instant joy!

gap wedge: A short club with a launch angle that falls between your pitching wedge and sand wedge.

garbage: a generic term used to describe small side bets on each hole. For example, a "greeny" is won when, on a par 3 hole, a player's drive lands on the green, and par is made.

greens in regulation: Refers to the number of strokes needed to reach a green in order to two-putt and make par. For example, on a par 5 hole, making the "greens in regulation" means that you got on the green in three strokes; on a par 4, it's getting on the green in two strokes, etcetera.

greeny: Occurs on a par 3 hole when a player's drive lands (and remains) on the green, and then the player putts for par.

handicap: An index, computed semimonthly by the USGA, that is based upon eighteen-hole scores (minimum of ten rounds). It assumes that you enter your score for each completed round. Handicaps are a measure of skill level—the lower the handicap, the more skillful the player.

hazard: A course obstacle (water, swamp, woods, etcetera) defined by red or yellow stakes. Depending upon the hazard, a penalty stroke and/or certain restrictions are imposed. For example, when hitting from inside a yellow hazard you are not permitted to ground your club.

hybrid club: A club, usually the equivalent to a 4-, 5-, 6-, or 7-iron that merges the best qualities of an iron and fairway wood/ metal.

junk: A generic term used to describe small side bets on each hole. See "garbage" for an example.

Krone factor: Hitting the ball on a wider path than you believe is necessary when putting on lengthy sidewise slope.

lob: a highly lofted shot, usually produced by a wedge.

lob wedge: A short club with a launch angle greater than your sand wedge.

long putter: A putter that is longer than a belly putter, often reaching shoulder level.

match play: Scoring golf by counting the number of holes won, rather than the number of strokes used.

nassau: Sounds like a town in the Bahamas, but in this book it refers to a betting game in which the front nine, back nine, and the entire eighteen holes represents separate bets.

negative self-talks: Unvoiced thoughts about fears/concerns that occur when you have a bad shot or when you are confronted with a challenging hazard.

positive images: Recalling in your "mind's eye" a visualization of a specific successful shot that you made.

rough: Grassy areas off the fairway, with higher blades of grass, usually making it more difficult to hit a clean shot.

sandy: Occurs when a player hits out of a bunker and putts his next shot into the cup for a par.

swish shot: A shot designed to produce a high trajectory and backspin. Useful when having to hit the green when a hazard (such as a bunker) is between your ball and the green (see chapter 4).

target line: Refers to an imaginary line between the ball's location and the pin that a golfer believes will result in the ball being holed.

unplayable lie: A declaration made by a player when his/her ball is resting in a spot that is difficult or impossible to hit. For example, at the base of a tree with the ball nestled between above-ground roots or in thick woods that do not permit swinging a club.

wormburner: A ball struck (usually topped) so that it runs rapidly along the ground.

yips: Short, jerky motions with hands or arms (usually when putting) that hinder a smooth stroke.